Great
SHAK
The Science of **Earthquakes**

thquakes . . . **HEADLINE SCIENCE** . . . Earthquakes . . . Headline Science . . . Earthquakes . . .

by Darlene R. Stille

Content Adviser:
Gary Lewis, Education & Outreach,
Geological Society of America

Science Adviser:
Terrence E. Young Jr., M.Ed., M.L.S.,
Jefferson Parish (Louisiana) Public School System

Reading Adviser:
Rosemary G. Palmer, Ph.D., Department of Literacy,
College of Education, Boise State University

Compass Point Books • 151 Good Counsel Drive, P. O. Box 669 • Mankato, MN 56002-0669

 This book was manufactured with paper containing
at least 10 percent post-consumer waste.

Library of Congress Cataloging-in-Publication Data
Stille, Darlene R.
  Great shakes : the science of earthquakes / by Darlene R. Stille.
     p. cm.—(Headline)
  Includes index.
  ISBN 978-0-7565-3947-4 (library binding)
  ISBN 978-0-7565-3368-7 (paperback)
 1. Earthquakes—Juvenile literature. I. Title. II. Series.
  QE521.3.S757 2008
  551.22—dc22   2008005739

Editor: Anthony Wacholtz
Designers: Ellen Schofield and Ashlee Suker
Page Production: Ashlee Suker
Photo Researcher: Eric Gohl
Cartographer: XNR Productions, Inc.
Illustrator: Eric Hoffmann

Art Director: LuAnn Ascheman-Adams
Creative Director: Keith Griffin
Editorial Director: Nick Healy
Managing Editor: Catherine Neitge

Photographs ©: Warrick Page/Getty Images, cover (bottom); Marvin Sperlin/iStockphoto, cover
(inset, left), 11; Robert Van Beets/iStockphoto, cover (inset, middle); Furchin/iStockphoto, cover
(inset, right); jirijura/Shutterstock, 2; AP Images/Greg Baker, 5; David Hume Kennerly/Getty Images,
7; Jes Aznar/AFP/Getty Images, 8 (top); AFP/Getty Images, 8 (bottom); David McNew/Newsmak-
ers/Getty Images, 12; David Paul Morris/Getty Images, 14; Jay Directo/AFP/Getty Images, 15; Gary
Hincks/Photo Researchers, Inc, 16, 22; Library of Congress, 19; Kevin Schafer/Alamy, 20; AP Images/
Gary Kazanjian, 21, 30; Spencer Platt/Getty Images, 23, 25; AP Images, 28; David R. Frazier Photoli-
brary, Inc./Alamy, 32; AP Images/Daniel R. Patmore, 33; AP Images/Murad Sezer, 34; AP Images/Rick
Smith, 36; Henry Westheim Photography/Alamy, 37; Business Wire/Getty Images, 38; Joel Nito/AFP/
Getty Images, 39; Alan Levenson/Time Life Pictures/Getty Images, 40; China Photos/Getty Images,
41; Yoshikazu Tsuno/AFP/Getty Images, 42; AP Images/Ben Margot, 43.

Visit Compass Point Books on the Internet at *www.compasspointbooks.com*
or e-mail your request to *custserv@compasspointbooks.com*

CHINA STRUGGLES TO SHELTER MILLIONS OF QUAKE'S HOMELESS

The New York Times
May 25, 2008

Two weeks after a powerful earthquake devastated parts of southwest China, the government is struggling to deal with a crisis that has left up to five million people homeless. Beijing is urgently appealing for international aid, including tents and other supplies to house, feed and clothe residents in an area that is roughly the size of Massachusetts, Vermont, New Hampshire and New Jersey combined. ...

The appeals came as the death toll in the May 12 earthquake, the country's worst natural disaster in more than three decades, was raised to 62,000 people, with more than 350,000 injured and about 23,000 still missing.

On May 12, 2008, a devastating 7.9-magnitude earthquake struck southwestern China. The earthquake occurred in the middle of the day, while many people were at work or attending school. Buildings in the region were destroyed before many of the people could escape.

Following the earthquake, the chaos continued. Powerful aftershocks shook the area for more than two weeks after the first earthquake, making it dangerous to search for survivors. The earthquake weakened several dams in the area, and about 150,000 people were evacuated. And with so many people missing, the death toll continued to rise.

Soldiers in Beichuan searched the ruins of collapsed buildings for survivors of the massive 2008 earthquake in southwestern China.

KEEPING CURRENT

News changes every minute, and readers need access to the latest information to keep current. Here are a few key search terms to help you locate up-to-the-minute earthquake headlines:

EarthScope	earthquake warning system
earthquake facts and statistics	latest earthquakes
earthquake-proof buildings	San Andreas Fault Observatory at Depth
earthquake structural testing	U.S. Geological Survey

KILLER EARTHQUAKES

How much damage can an earthquake do? It depends on where it happens. For example, an earthquake centered in a rural area will probably not cause much damage. If the central part of the earthquake is close to a city, where many people live and work in buildings, the damage is likely to be great.

The amount of damage caused by an earthquake can also be related to the type of ground on which a structure is built. For example, buildings on sand or mud will not be as stable in an earthquake as those built on solid rock.

The timing of an earthquake is also important. A powerful earthquake struck Northridge, California, a suburb of Los Angeles, on January 17, 1994, just before dawn. Most of the residents were asleep in their beds. At around 4:30 A.M., books began to slide off of shelves, and dishes crashed to the floor. Outside, huge interstate highway overpasses swayed, big chunks of concrete pavement came thudding down, and the walls of buildings wobbled and collapsed. A powerful earthquake had set the earth around Los Angeles heaving and rolling. The quake only lasted 40 seconds, but that was enough time for it to kill about 60 people, injure more than 7,000 others, and cause billions of dollars in damage.

However, it could have been worse. "If this had happened in the middle of the day we would have been stacking up the bodies," said a Los Angeles firefighter. There were few vehicles on the highways when the Northridge earthquake struck, and only a small number of people were threatened by falling debris on the streets.

Vehicles were stranded on a bridge in Northridge, California, after an earthquake caused sections of the bridge to collapse.

EARTHQUAKE POWER

Some quakes are very powerful. The shaking they cause can be felt for thousands of miles. Other earthquakes are very weak and can only be detected with instruments.

Seismologists—scientists who study earthquakes and the waves they produce—use a scale called magnitude, or moment magnitude, to tell how powerful an earthquake is. It measures physical features such as the energy released when rock along a fault moves.

Jane Punongbayan of the Philippine Institute of
Volcanology and Seismology analyzes the lines
on a seismograph showing the intensity of
a 6.0-magnitude earthquake in late 2007.

Moment magnitude is one scale that scientists use to measure the power of an earthquake. They also use two other scales, which are named after the scientists who invented them: the Richter scale and the Mercalli scale.

The Richter scale, named after U.S. seismologist Charles Richter, uses numbers to rate the strength of each earthquake. Numbers close to 0 are for weak earthquakes. The strongest

9.5 QUAKE

The most powerful earthquake ever recorded struck Chile in 1960. Geologists found that the quake was a magnitude 9.5. About 2,000 people were killed, 3,000 were injured, and 2 million were left homeless. The earthquake resulted in $550 million in damage. Hawaii, the Philippines, and the West Coast of the United States also felt the effects of the monstrous quake.

THE RICHTER SCALE

An increase of 1.0 on the Richter scale equals 10 times the destructive power and 32 times the amount of energy released during an earthquake. A 7.0 earthquake is 10 times more powerful than a 6.0 earthquake and releases 32 times more energy. However, the same earthquake is 100 times more powerful than a 5.0 earthquake and releases 1,024 times more energy. Many seismologists believe the destructive power of an earthquake is better measured by the amount of energy released.

Magnitude	Possible effects	Average number/year
1	detectable only by instruments	unknown
2	barely detectable	1.3 million
3	felt indoors	130,000
4	felt by most people; slight damage	13,000
5	felt by all; damage minor to moderate	1,319
6	moderately destructive	134
7	major damage	17
8	total destruction	1

Sources: United States Geological Survey
   Science and Technology Department of the Carnegie Library of Pittsburgh. *The Handy Science Answer Book*. Detroit: Visible Ink Press, 1997.

earthquakes are assigned an 8 or higher, with no upper limit to the scale.

The moment magnitude scale was developed in 1979 and is based on the Richter scale. Geologists today usually use the moment magnitude scale. However, because the moment magnitude is more complex, geologists will translate an earthquake's rating to the Richter scale for the general public.

Unlike the Richter scale, the Mercalli scale, named after Italian volcanologist Giuseppe Mercalli, does not measure the magnitude of an earthquake. It describes the destruction an earthquake causes. This scale has 12 categories that describe how an earthquake feels. It depends on people, not instruments, to make the observations. ◤

2006 TECTONIC PLATE MOTION REVERSAL NEAR ACAPULCO PUZZLES EARTHQUAKE SCIENTISTS

»» Science Daily
August 6, 2007

Instead of creeping toward Mexico City at about one inch (2.54 centimeters) per year—the expected speed from plate tectonic theory—the region near Acapulco moved in the opposite direction for six months and sped up by four times, said CU-Boulder aerospace engineering Professor Kristine Larson.

"The million-dollar question is whether the event makes a major earthquake in the region less likely or more likely," said Larson, whose research is funded in part by the National Science Foundation. "So far, it does not appear to be reducing the earthquake hazard."

How can mountains and other features on Earth move? They sit on gigantic slabs of rock called tectonic plates that slowly but constantly move. Although geologists know there is a direct connection between earthquakes and the movements of the plates, they want to learn more about the forces created by this movement.

Until the early 2000s, researchers could not accurately measure how much a particular mountain moves. But now they can monitor the precise movement of Earth's crust.

Research stations contain electronic equipment that picks up signals from satellites orbiting Earth. The satellites are part of the Global

A GPS instrument was set up by members of the United States Geological Society (USGS) to map fault movements in northern California.

Positioning System. This system helps airplanes and ships pinpoint where they are any place on Earth. The system also watches the gradual movement of mountains. People can buy GPS screens for their cars to get directions.

"We can measure movement [in the earth] as small as a few millimeters a year with very portable GPS instruments," said geologist Frank Webb of NASA's Jet Propulsion Laboratory. The Southern California project was completed in 2001. Since then, high-tech GPS systems have been widely used to study Earth's surface.

Seismic readings along a fault on Mammoth Mountain in California had geologists monitoring the area for volcanic activity.

WHAT CAUSES AN EARTHQUAKE?

Earthquakes are caused by sudden movements of the rock in Earth's crust. This movement happens along a crack in the rock called a fault. A fault is a fracture, or break, between two blocks of rock in Earth's crust. Most earthquakes begin in faults deep below Earth's surface. The point at which movement on the fault begins is called the focus. The point on the surface directly above the focus is called the epicenter.

Extremely powerful earthquakes usually only occur once a year or so. On the other hand, smaller earthquakes occur hundreds of times a day, but most are so weak that they can only be detected by equipment. Earthquakes often occur in groups called swarms or clusters. The most powerful earthquake in a cluster is the mainshock. Foreshocks come before the mainshock, and aftershocks follow the mainshock. Foreshocks and aftershocks are usually smaller quakes, but they can still cause damage. The aftershocks can last for several weeks after the earthquake.

The destruction that results from an earthquake occurs because of sudden movements in the rock along a fault. These movements send out waves that travel through rock and soil in all directions, causing the ground to shift and shake. The more forcefully the rock moves and the farther the crack travels, the more powerful the earthquake will be.

Whether an earthquake will be weak or powerful also depends on how deep the focus is. The focus can be hundreds of miles deep, but these quakes do not usually cause much damage. Earthquakes with a focus close to the surface are much worse. The focus of the Northridge earthquake, for example, was only 11 miles (18.4 kilometers) below the surface. The source of this violent shaking and destruction is directly related to the movement of tectonic plates.

NOW YOU KNOW

Japan is one of the most earthquake-prone nations in the world. Thousands of earthquakes occur in Japan every year, but most of them are very weak.

PLATE TECTONICS

Tectonic plates make up Earth's crust, the top layer of Earth. The crust is a cold, solid layer of rock and soil. There are three more layers under the crust: the mantle, the outer core, and the inner core. The mantle is made of hot, soft rock. The plates slowly slide around on the mantle.

Earthquakes occur at plate boundaries, the places where the plates meet. There are three types of boundaries: divergent, convergent, and transform.

Divergent boundaries are places where plates are moving away from each other. Melted rock called magma oozes up from the mantle and cools, forming new crust at the edges of the plates.

Convergent boundaries are places where plates are coming together. Sometimes the edges of colliding plates crunch up to form mountains. Other times, the edge of one plate slides under the edge of the other plate. This edge plunges downward and melts in the hot mantle.

In Parkfield, California—a city known as "The Earthquake Capital of the World"— a bridge spans two tectonic plates.

Transform boundaries are places where plates are sliding past one another. There is a transform boundary along the California coast. There the Pacific Plate slowly grinds northwestward past the North American Plate.

Most faults form in the rock near plate boundaries. As the huge plates grind along, blocks of rock on the faults can get stuck. Still the huge plates continue to move. Strain builds up along the fault until suddenly the rocks break free. When the rocks break, they release energy that sends seismic waves through the earth. The shaking caused by these waves is what people feel as an earthquake.

Although most faults occur on the edges of tectonic plates, faults can also occur in the middle of tectonic plates. These rare intra-plate faults can cause intra-plate quakes that are quite powerful. For example, an intra-plate quake occurred in Australia in 1989. Measuring 5.6 on the Richter scale, it killed 13 people and caused about $1 billion in damages. Scientists are trying to learn more about how intra-plate faults occur and what triggers earthquakes along them.

THE RING OF FIRE

More earthquakes occur around a large part of the Pacific Ocean than any other place in the world. This area around the Pacific Ocean is called the Ring of Fire. It goes along the Pacific coastlines of North and South America, past Alaska and eastern Russia, and through the Philippines and Indonesia. The Ring of Fire was named for the many volcanoes that erupt there.

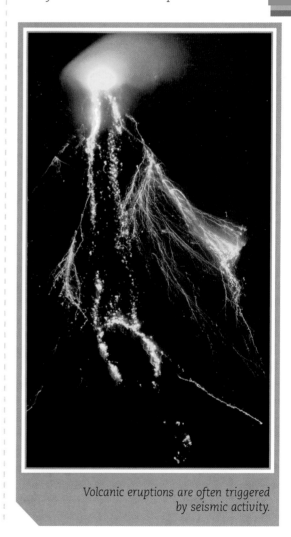

Volcanic eruptions are often triggered by seismic activity.

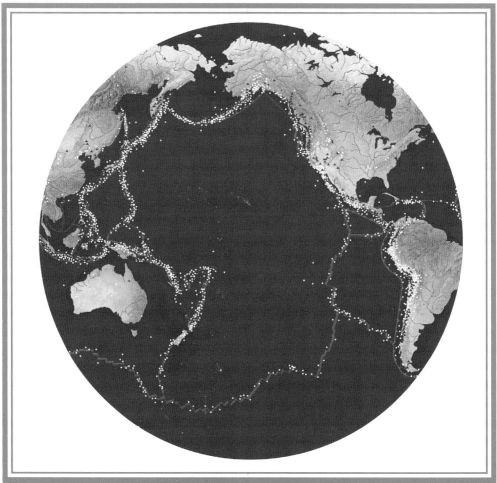

Earthquakes (yellow) and volcanoes (red triangles) frequently occur near the Ring of Fire.

There is a link between earthquakes and volcanoes. Magma often oozes up near the edge of a plate that is sinking and melting. In some places, the magma pushes through the crust, forming volcanoes. Movements of the plates that carry the Pacific Ocean floor can cause volcanoes to form on land or under water. The plate movements also set off earthquakes along the many faults in this region. ◼

MAJOR EARTHQUAKE DUE TO HIT SOUTHERN CALIFORNIA

National Geographic News
June 21, 2006

About 300 years of pent-up stress in southern California is sufficient to trigger a catastrophic earthquake on the San Andreas Fault system, according to a new study. ...

The fault is notorious for major earthquakes, including the 1906 earthquake that reduced the San Francisco Bay Area to piles of smoldering rubble.

But the 100-mile (160-kilometer) southern section of the fault, which runs south from San Bernardino to the east of Los Angeles and San Diego, has remained eerily quiet for nearly three centuries.

Now, scientists believe, the fault is ready to rumble.

HOW FAULT MOVEMENT CAUSES EARTHQUAKES

Tectonic plates are always slowly moving. The Pacific Plate, for example, moves northwestward at a rate of about 2 3/5 inches (7 cm) a year. Sometimes the rock along a fault moves steadily as well. This type of fault movement is called creep. The creep rate of many faults is about 1/5 inches (5 millimeters) a year.

Sometimes the blocks of rock along a fault become locked and do not move at all. Because the plates continue to move, strain builds up along the fault. Suddenly, part of the fault gives way and the rock moves. During the 1906 San Francisco earthquake, one section of fault moved more than 20 feet (6 meters) in a matter of seconds. As a result of this sudden movement, the ground began to shake and a great earthquake occurred.

HOW GEOLOGISTS CLASSIFY EARTHQUAKE FAULTS

Not all faults are alike. Faults may or may not be visible on the ground surface. Many are deep within Earth's crust. Some faults are only a few inches long, while others are hundreds of miles long. The San Andreas is one of the longest fault zones in the world.

The San Andreas is made up of many faults. It is on the boundary between the Pacific Plate and the North American Plate. The Pacific Plate moves northwestward past the North American Plate, causing many earthquakes along the San Andreas Fault. This sudden movement of rock along the San Andreas caused a powerful earthquake in 1906 that destroyed much of San Francisco.

NOW YOU KNOW

In 2006, geologists found three new faults in Northern California. The faults run under small towns and vineyards in Mendocino County.

The shaking from the 1906 San Francisco earthquake destroyed many homes and businesses, but it was the resulting fires that ruined much of the city.

Geologists group faults according to the angle of the break in the rock. Sometimes the fracture goes straight down and forms a 90-degree angle with the horizontal layer of rock underground. This kind of fracture looks like a T. Fractures, however, can be at any angle. Geologists call the angle of the fault the dip.

Faults are also grouped according to how the rock on each side of the fracture moves. The rock can move right or left, up or down. Geologists call faults in which the rock on either side moves up and down dip-slip faults.

There are three main types of faults—normal, thrust (or reverse), and strike-slip. Some faults lie close to the surface. Others lie in layers of rock deep underground.

In a normal fault, the block on one side of the fault drops below the rock on the other side. In a thrust fault, one block of rock is pushed above the rock on the other side.

In strike-slip faults, the rock on each side moves sideways. A side of the fault can move either to the right or to the left. If a person stood on either side of the fault and watched it move during an earthquake, the other side would appear to move to the right.

One of the most famous strike-slip faults is the San Andreas Fault. The entire fault zone runs more than 800 miles (1,280 km) from San Francisco through southern California to Mexico.

EARTHQUAKE STRAIN

Geophysicists who study faults are especially interested in the data from instruments called strainmeters. The moving tectonic plates create a force that stretches and squeezes the rock around faults. This stretching and squeezing produces very slight motion that cannot be detected by seismographs.

A laser strainmeter can detect this slight motion. It measures tiny changes in distance along a beam of laser light that travels in a vacuum through a long tube. Other strainmeters are placed in holes bored in the ground. They measure changes in the diameter of the hole.

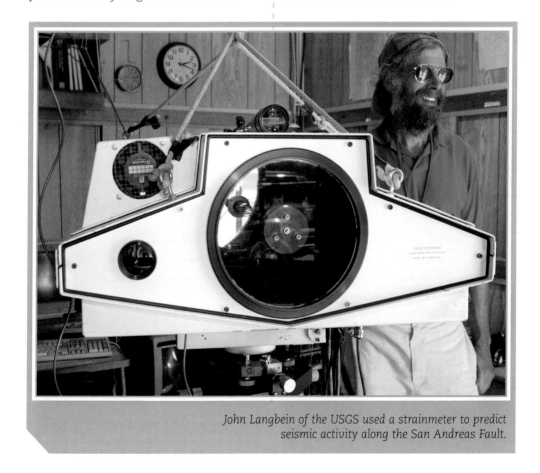

John Langbein of the USGS used a strainmeter to predict seismic activity along the San Andreas Fault.

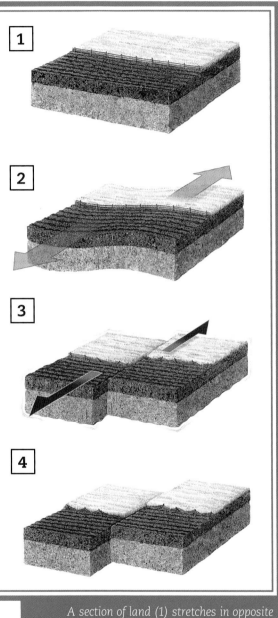

A section of land (1) stretches in opposite directions (2) during elastic rebound. When the pressure becomes too great (3), the land splits in two (4).

ELASTIC STRAIN

Moving plates tug on the stuck rock along a fault. This tugging builds up a type of energy in the rock called elastic strain energy. Elastic strain changes the shape of the rock along the fault.

Think of what happens to a rubber band when you pull on it. As elastic strain builds up, the material becomes longer and thinner. When too much elastic strain builds up, the rubber band breaks, energy is released, and the rubber band snaps back. This snapping back is called elastic rebound.

A similar thing happens to rock along a fault. Friction between the two sides of the fault locks the rock in place. When enough strain builds up, the rock suddenly moves and releases elastic strain energy. The energy sets off seismic waves in the earth, causing the ground to shake. After the blocks of rock move, each block snaps back to its original shape. After an earthquake, the cycle starts over. The strain caused by the moving tectonic plates once again begins to build up along the fault.

HEADLINE SCIENCE

John Taber of the Museum of Natural History in New York City explained how the museum's earthquake station monitors seismic activity in three regions: Fairbanks, Alaska; Tucson, Arizona; and Nagano, Japan.

SEEING INTO EARTH

Astronomers use telescopes to see far out into space, and biologists use microscopes to see tiny organisms. Geophysicists can "see inside" the planet, however, by using the instruments of EarthScope—a program that monitors the processes of earthquakes and volcanoes.

GPS receivers are a major part of EarthScope. The receivers can watch for movement along plate boundaries. Portable and permanent seismometers are also used by EarthScope to monitor earthquake activity all over the North American continent.

"It's like a ship of discovery," says geophysicist Robert Smith, of the University of Utah, in describing EarthScope. "This is the first time we've had this enormous capability of modern instruments that we're going to be able to put it all together in one picture."

FINALLY, A SOLID LOOK AT EARTH'S CORE

>>> Live Science
April 14, 2005

Scientists have long thought Earth's core is solid. Now they have some solid evidence.

The core is thought to be a two-part construction. The inner core is solid iron, and that's surround[ed] by a molten core, theory holds. Around the core is the mantle, and near the planet's surface is a thin crust—the part that breaks now and then and creates earthquakes.

A study announced today involved complex monitoring of seismic waves passing through the planet. The technique is not new, but this is the first time it's been employed so effectively to probe the heart of our world.

Seismic waves are important tools for geologists. Studying these waves helps them learn about Earth's interior. Scientists use seismic waves to "see" inside Earth in much the way that doctors use X-rays and CT scans to "see" inside the body. The technique used to study Earth's core is based on the fact that there are different kinds of seismic waves. Some waves can move through liquids, such as the outer core, and some can only move through solids, such as the inner core.

EARTHQUAKE WAVES

The energy released when rock along a fault breaks produces several types of seismic waves. Geologists group the waves into two main categories —body waves and surface waves. Body waves travel directly through the planet. Surface waves only move along Earth's surface.

There are two types of body waves— P (primary) waves and S (secondary) waves. P waves are the fastest moving body waves, moving out from the

At the Planet Earth exhibit at the Museum of Natural History in New York City, a large screen displays a real-time map that monitors the presence of seismic waves across the world.

earthquake's focus at speeds of up to 4 miles (7 km) per second. P waves travel through solid rock, melted rock, or liquids. P waves move through the earth in the way that sound waves move through air. Each wave compresses and expands the rock or liquid as it passes through. These are the first waves to reach the surface. Some P waves are so powerful they will produce a loud roar when they break the surface.

S waves go out from the focus next, and they move much more slowly than P waves. They move the rock up and down or from side to side as they pass through the planet. S waves are like waves that move along a rope or hose when it is wiggled. S waves can only move through solid rock and not through any type of liquid. Because they can move vertically or horizontally, however, they are more destructive than P waves.

There are also two types of surface waves that only travel through Earth's crust—Love waves and Rayleigh waves. Similar to the way a snake crawls along the ground, Love waves,

named after A.E.H. Love, move from side to side. Rayleigh waves, named after Lord John William Strutt Rayleigh, behave like water waves that roll through Earth's surface. This motion makes the ground move up and down and from side to side. Rayleigh waves cause most of the ground shaking and damage from an earthquake.

WHAT WAVES TELL ABOUT EARTHQUAKES

Geologists use seismographs to detect earthquake waves. Seismographs once worked somewhat like old fax machines. When an earthquake

Shock waves produced by Rayleigh waves can travel far enough upward to cause a disturbance in the iono-sphere—a layer of Earth's atmosphere about 50 to 300 miles (80 to 480 km) above Earth's surface.

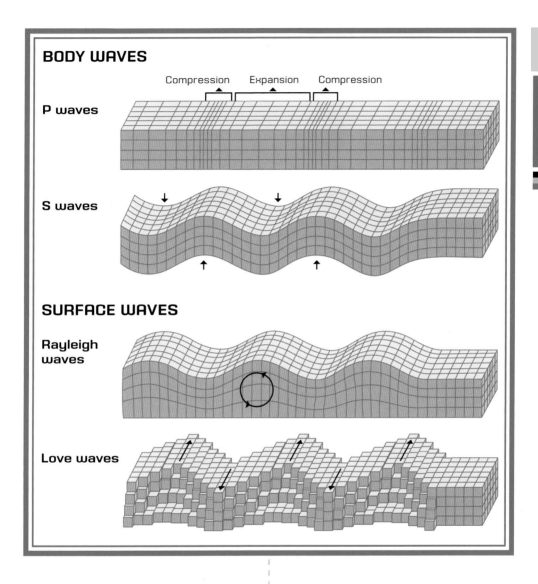

BODY WAVES

P waves

Compression   Expansion   Compression

S waves

SURFACE WAVES

Rayleigh waves

Love waves

caused the ground under the seismograph to shake, heated needles moved up and down to make lines on a drum of heat-sensitive paper. Modern seismographs use digital technology to transmit signals from earthquake detectors in the ground to recorders that can be hundreds of miles away.

Seismographs produce seismograms, which look like squiggly lines

Lu Pei-ling, an official from Taiwan's Central Weather Bureau, studied the readings from a seismograph following a 6.7-magnitude earthquake in December 2006.

on a roll of paper. The lines represent seismic waves. Scientists use seismograms to tell when and where an earthquake occurred. They also use the waves to determine how powerful an earthquake is.

The speed of the waves helps them determine where the epicenter is located. P waves are the first waves to reach the seismograph, and S waves arrive next. Seismologists use this time delay to calculate how far the earthquake's epicenter is from the seismograph. They subtract the time when the last S wave arrived from the time the first P wave arrived. Then they multiply this figure by 5 miles (8 km) per second to find out how far away the epicenter is.

Seismologists need data from seismographs in three locations to find the epicenter of the earthquake. They draw three circles on a map that show the distance of the quake from the seismograph. The point where all three circles intersect is the epicenter of the quake. Computers that have data from three or more seismographs can more accurately figure the exact location of the epicenter.

SAN ANDREAS FAULT OBSERVATORY AT DEPTH REVEALS NEW INSIGHTS INT THE "EARTHQUAKE MACHINE

Science Daily
December 15, 2005

The San Andreas Fault Observatory at Depth (SAFOD)—
the first underground observatory to provide physica
samples and real-time seismological data from deep
inside an active fault zone—is yielding surprising new
clues about the origin of earthquakes. SAFOD is a
major research component of EarthScope, a Nationa
Science Foundation-funded program being carried out in
collaboration with the U.S. Geological Survey (USGS) to
investigate the forces that shape the North American
continent and the physical processes controlling
earthquakes and volcanic eruptions.

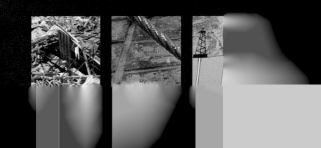

Earthquake scientists dream of being able to predict when and where an earthquake will strike. The ability to predict an earthquake could save thousands of lives, but this is not an easy task. In fact, seismologists do not even like to use the term predict.

Contractors drilled a hole more than a mile deep near the San Andreas Fault, allowing seismologists to plant instruments and equipment beneath the surface.

Instead, they talk about earthquake forecasting. While weather forecasters figure the odds of rain falling in a certain place on a certain day, earthquake forecasters figure the odds of an earthquake happening in a certain place during a certain time period.

WHERE WILL AN EARTHQUAKE STRIKE?

Scientists in the 1920s were the first to notice that most earthquakes happen in certain places. They now know that these earthquake zones are near the edges of two or more moving tectonic plates.

Seismologists are certain that a major earthquake will soon occur within the Ring of Fire, where 90 percent of all earthquakes occur. A big earthquake is also likely to occur in a region called the Alpide Belt, the second most active earthquake zone. Many deadly earthquakes have struck countries that border the Alpide Belt, including Turkey, India, and Pakistan. In addition, future earthquakes will occur in rift valleys and along mid-

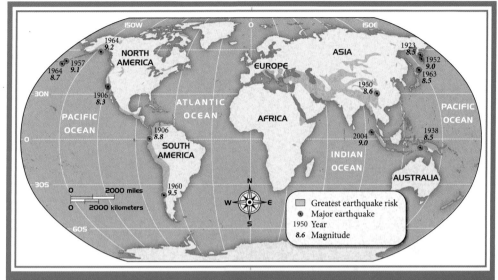

Cities with the greatest earthquake risk include San Francisco; Los Angeles; Mexico City; Rome, Italy; Athens, Greece; Istanbul, Turkey; Cairo, Egypt; Jakarta, Indonesia; Manila, the Philippines; Tehran, Iran; Tokyo, Japan; and Hong Kong and Beijing, China.

ocean ridges where tectonic plates are continually moving apart. Africa's Great Rift Valley is a major earthquake zone. Rift valleys can be on land or under the ocean.

Areas that are on or near faults in an earthquake zone are more likely to suffer a major quake. Scientists study the history of quakes along a fault to forecast the chance of a major earthquake occurring at a certain place in the fault zone.

MYSTERIOUS FAULT

Most people living in the Midwestern United States feel safe from earthquakes even though they might not really be safe. Three powerful earthquakes with a magnitude of 8 on the Richter scale rocked the central Midwest in the winter of 1811 and 1812. The quakes shook up the 400 residents of New Madrid in what is now the state of Missouri, but little damage was done because few people lived in the area.

The energy waves, however, caused church bells to ring in Boston about 1,000 miles (1,600 km) away. The earthquakes also caused major geological changes. Areas of land sank as much as 20 inches (50 cm) into the ground, creating several new lake beds. Because of the shifting land, sections of the Mississippi River briefly flowed in the opposite direction.

What if a similar quake occurred in New Madrid today? It could cause major damage to cities from St. Louis to Memphis, Tennessee. It might even be felt in Chicago.

The 1811 and 1812 quakes occurred along the New Madrid Fault and other faults nearby, but geologists do not yet completely understand what created these faults. Geologists have discovered strong magnetic forces in the region that are produced by igneous rock. Igneous rock forms when magma builds up from inside Earth, then cools and hardens. Igneous rock is found in regions where plates are moving apart. Therefore, geologists suspect that North America contains a "failed rift." At

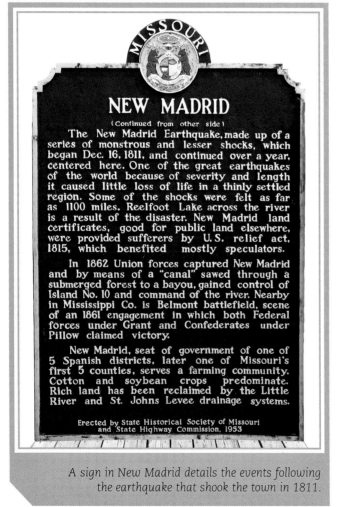

A sign in New Madrid details the events following the earthquake that shook the town in 1811.

some point in the past, the plate movement stopped, and over millions of years, sediments covered the rift. The plate movement left behind a series of faults that could move again. If they do, it would set off earthquakes as powerful as the ones that shook the Midwest in the early 1800s.

Powerful earthquakes still occur in the Midwest. On April 18, 2008, a 5.2-magnitude earthquake shook the small town of West Salem, Illinois. The earthquake caused buildings to shake in Chicago—230 miles (368 km) away. This was the strongest earthquake in southern Illinois in 40 years.

A resident of Mount Carmel, Illinois, views the damage to her house following the earthquake that struck the Midwest in April 2008.

A woman searched for belongings from her house amidst the rubble that resulted from the earthquake in Turkey in August 1999.

WHEN WILL AN EARTHQUAKE OCCUR?

It is difficult to figure the odds of a major earthquake occurring in a certain place, but it is even more difficult to predict a certain time. In general, the longer it has been since a major quake occurred along a fault, the more likely it is that one will soon happen.

Sections of rock along the southern part of the San Andreas Fault zone have not had a major break in about 300 years. The gigantic tectonic plates keep moving, however, and strain builds up along the edges of the fault. Seismologists predict that the rock will break sometime before 2030. This break would trigger powerful earthquakes in southern California.

After seismologists forecast a quake along the Anatolian Fault zone that runs through Turkey, there were several major quakes in that region. In 1996, seismologists forecast that the city of Izmit, Turkey, would experience an earthquake greater than magnitude 6.7 within the next 30 years. In 1999, a 7.8-magnitude earthquake set the city shaking, killing about 17,500 people and leaving another 500,000 people homeless.

ENGINEERS WORK ON QUAKE-PROOF BUILDINGS

>> Lehigh University
April 18, 2006

At Lehigh University, home of one of the largest structural testing facilities in the United States, scientists have tested a next-generation "self-centering" system that uses gigantic steel bands to hold building columns and beams in place during an earthquake. ...

The system has shown promise in testing. In a hangar-sized lab just south of Bethlehem [Pennsylvania], gigantic hydraulic pistons subjected a building frame to about 50 percent more force than was generated by the 1906 San Francisco quake. Aside from some popped bolts which engineers designed to have happen, the frame emerged unscathed.

Millions of people live in places where earthquakes occur. Those who live in earthquake-prone zones can suffer destruction from the ground shaking as well as from landslides, mudslides, and giant waves called tsunamis. Tsunamis set off by an underwater earthquake in 2005 killed more than 200,000 people in Indonesia. In addition, earthquakes can rupture water and gas lines. Ruptured gas lines set off fires that almost destroyed San Francisco in

Scientists at the ATLSS Engineering Research Center at Lehigh University tested new building materials created to endure the shaking caused by an earthquake.

1906. Firefighters could not put out the blaze because the quake also ruptured the city's water lines.

People near a fault can sometimes experience hardships caused by subsidence, the sinking of an area of ground. Subsidence can destroy structures such as roads, bridges, and dams.

Scientists and engineers want to protect people from future earthquakes and the damage they can cause. Engineers are working to create buildings that can withstand earthquakes. Scientists are working on early warning systems and on developing ways for people to protect themselves during an earthquake.

In September 1999, roads throughout Taiwan were mangled by an earthquake measuring 7.3 on the Richter scale.

DAMAGE AND SOIL TYPE

Scientists study soil type to determine how much damage an earthquake might cause. Houses, schools, offices, bridges, and other structures are more likely to suffer damage in certain areas of a city, depending on where they are built. Structures built on solid

In 2006, structural engineers from the University of San Diego, California, constructed a seven-story building that remained standing after a simulated earthquake.

rock have the best chance of escaping serious damage.

S waves travel faster through certain soil types. Solid rock does not move very much when S waves pass through. Looser soil particles move more, and very sandy soil moves the most. Seismic waves can make sandy soil behave like a liquid. This process is called liquefaction.

Entire parts of Port Royal, Jamaica, disappeared during an earthquake in 1692. Many Port Royal buildings were set on sand, so when the earthquake struck, the ground acted like liquid and the buildings sank into the ground. Much of old Port Royal is now under the sea.

Engineers examine the soil in places where earthquakes are likely to occur. They can also study the ground where a skyscraper or bridge is to be built and determine whether it is safe to build there.

QUAKE-RESISTANT BUILDINGS

Engineers say there is no such thing as a "quake-proof" building. An earthquake can damage even well-built structures. Still, engineers can design structures so that people inside have a good chance of surviving an earthquake.

Quake-resistant buildings already exist in San

Francisco, Tokyo, and other places that frequently experience earthquakes. Some of these buildings have extra steel girders that help keep the buildings from swaying so much that they could fall down when the ground

Iron casing was used to reinforce the concrete in a major bridge in Manila, the Philippines.

A series of robotic systems wound carbon fiber thread around highway columns near San Diego for extra support and to prevent damage from an earthquake.

shakes. Some structures have concrete reinforced with steel bars that help prevent the concrete from breaking up.

Other structures have "shock absorbers" that go in the ground under buildings or bridges and separate the structure from the shaking ground. The shock absorbers can be rubber pads, steel rollers, or springs that are designed to absorb the energy from S waves.

EARTHQUAKE WARNING SYSTEMS

Scientists are working to develop earthquake warning systems. Some places in Japan, Mexico, and Turkey have such warning systems. In 2006, the USGS began testing a warning system for California. It accurately forecast an earthquake felt in San Francisco in October 2007 a few seconds before the ground began to shake.

These systems detect the first P waves created by an earthquake. The systems could set off warning sirens or send other signals to utility companies.

Safety officials say that a warning of even a few seconds could save lives. Train operators could put on the brakes to prevent the train from derailing, gas companies could shut down gas pipes, and electric companies could cut off power. People could seek safe places in homes, schools, and office buildings.

As a precaution against aftershocks following a 5.7-magnitude earthquake in 2005, students in Ruichang, China, attended classes outside.

As part of a nationwide earthquake drill in Japan, children wearing flameproof hoods were led from their classroom. More than 2 million people participate in the drill each year.

PREPARING FOR AN EARTHQUAKE

Public safety officials say every person in an earthquake-prone area should be prepared for a major quake. They advise people to:

- Have a three-day supply of food, water, and medicines
- Know where your home's shutoffs are for water, gas, and electricity
- Locate the safest room for shelter from falling objects
- Be familiar with all exits from a home, school, or office
- Know where the nearest fire and police stations are
- Make sure all family members have an identification card

During an earthquake, safety officials say, people should remember to duck, cover, and hold. First, duck under a sturdy structure, such as a doorway or a table, to prevent heavy items from falling on you. Then, with one hand, cover your head for extra protection. With the other hand, hold

A new, safer bridge was constructed in California in 2005. The bridge was built with state-of-the-art safety features that protect against the shaking of an earthquake.

on to something, such as the doorway or a table leg, to keep your balance.

Safety officials also say to stay away from heavy pieces of furniture, appliances, glass windowpanes, shelving, and anything made of plaster or brick, such as fireplaces. Hallways are usually the safest place to take cover. Kitchens and garages are the least safe because of falling objects and exposure to hazardous materials.

CHALLENGES OF EARTHQUAKE SCIENCE

Scientists are working to better understand earthquakes. They want to know more about the forces that cause them. These scientists have learned a great deal by studying seismic waves and changes in the rock along a fault. With new kinds of equipment—from orbiting satellites to electromagnetic detectors and computer models—they hope to better understand, and perhaps even forecast, future earthquakes. They believe that warnings based on better forecasts will help save lives.

1201
Earthquake in the eastern Mediterranean, labeled the worst earthquake in history, claims an estimated 1 million lives

1760
Geologist and English clergyman John Mitchell publishes his theory that the epicenter and speed of an earthquake can be calculated by measuring the times that two waves arrive at different locations

1811–1812
Major earthquakes shake areas in the Midwest near New Madrid in present-day Missouri

1855
Italian seismologist Luigi Palmieri invents the first instrument capable of recording the time, intensity, and length of an earthquake

1857
Irish engineer Robert Mallet develops the first earthquake map, which shows that earthquakes occur more frequently in certain locations around the world

1902
Italian seismologist Giuseppe Mercalli invents the Mercalli scale for measuring the destructive power of an earthquake

1935
American seismologist Charles Richter invents the Richter scale, an earthquake measuring system that assigns numbers to earthquakes based on their strength and intensity

1960s
Seismographs are linked to form an earthquake-detecting network

1979
The moment magnitude scale is developed

1996
Scientists predict a major earthquake will occur in Turkey, which then happened in 1999

1999
GPS systems come into use for measuring movement of tectonic plates

2006
New earthquake-resistant building materials undergo testing; an earthquake in Japan causes more than $1 trillion in economic damage

2007
Earthquakes cause 712 deaths worldwide—the fewest number of casualties since 2000

2008
On May 12, a 7.9-magnitude earthquake strikes southwestern China

Timeline

GLOSSARY

body waves
seismic waves that travel through Earth; they include primary (P) waves and secondary (S) waves

core
innermost layer of Earth

crust
top, rigid layer of Earth

epicenter
place on Earth's surface above an earthquake's focus

fault
crack in the rock that forms Earth's crust

focus
point inside Earth where rock breaks, setting off an earthquake

liquefaction
during an earthquake, the process of soil becoming fluidlike and unstable

magma
melted rock inside Earth

magnitude
unit for measuring an earthquake's power

mantle
layer of hot, soft rock under Earth's crust

plate boundaries
places where two or more tectonic plates meet

seismic waves
waves created by an earthquake

seismograms
data produced by a seismograph

seismographs
instruments that detect earthquakes

seismologists
scientists who study waves created by earthquakes

strainmeters
instruments used for measuring strain built up in rock along a fault

surface waves
seismic waves that travel along Earth's surface; Love waves and Rayleigh waves are the two types of waves

tectonic plates
giant slabs of rock that make up Earth's crust

volcanoes
vents in Earth's crust through which magma escapes

FURTHER RESOURCES

ON THE WEB

For more information on this topic, use FactHound.

1. Go to *www.facthound.com*
2. Type in this book ID: 0756539471
3. Click on the *Fetch It* button.

FactHound will find the best Web sites for you.

FURTHER READING

Fradin, Dennis, and Judy Fradin. *Witness to Disaster: Earthquakes*. Washington, D.C., National Geographic Children's Books, 2008.

Nobleman, Marc Tyler. *The San Francisco Earthquake of 1906*. Minneapolis: Compass Point Books, 2007.

Yep, Laurence. *The Earth Dragon Awakes: The San Francisco Earthquake of 1906*. New York: HarperCollins, 2008.

Zannos, Susan. *Charles Richter and the Story of the Richter Scale*. Bear, Del.: Mitchell Lane Publishers, 2004.

LOOK FOR OTHER BOOKS IN THIS SERIES:

Climate Crisis: The Science of Global Warming

Cure Quest: The Science of Stem Cell Research

Goodbye, Gasoline: The Science of Fuel Cells

Nature Interrupted: The Science of Environmental Chain Reactions

Rise of the Thinking Machines: The Science of Robots

SOURCE NOTES

Chapter 1: Barboza, David. "China Struggles to Shelter Millions of Quake's Homeless." *The New York Times*. 26 May 2008. 3 June 2008. www.nytimes.com/2008/05/26/world/asia/26china.html?ref=asia

Chapter 2: "2006 Tectonic Plate Motion Reversal Near Acapulco Puzzles Earthquake Scientists." *ScienceDaily*. 6 Aug. 2007. 21 April 2007. www.sciencedaily.com/releases/2007/08/070802130847.htm

Chapter 3: Roach, John. "Major Earthquake Due to Hit Southern California, Study Says." *National Geographic News*. 21 June 2006. 2 June 2007. http://news.nationalgeographic.com/news/2006/06/060621-earthquakes.html

Chapter 4: Britt, Robert Roy. "Finally, a Solid Look at Earth's Core." *LiveScience*. 14 April 2005. 24 Aug. 2007. www.livescience.com/environment/050414_earth_core.html

Chapter 5: "San Andreas Fault Observatory at Depth Reveals New Insights Into the 'Earthquake Machine.'" *ScienceDaily*. 15 Dec. 2005. 19 July 2007. www.sciencedaily.com/releases/2005/12/051213082828.htm

Chapter 6: "Engineers Work on Quake-Proof Buildings." Lehigh University. 18 April 2006. 25 June 2007. www3.lehigh.edu/News/V2news_story. asp?iNewsID=1758&strBack=%2Fnews%2FV2news_archive. asp%3FiStoryType%3D15

ABOUT THE AUTHOR

Darlene R. Stille is a science writer and author of more than 80 books for young people. She grew up in Chicago and attended the University of Illinois, where she discovered her love of writing. She has received numerous awards for her work. She lives and writes in Michigan.

INDEX